CRIMINAL PROFILING

A FORENSIC AND CRIMINAL PSYCHOLOGY GUIDE TO FBI AND STATISTICAL PROFILING

CONNOR WHITELEY

ACKNOWLEDGMENTS

Thank you to all my readers without you I couldn't do
what I love.

i

INTRODUCTION

Whenever people think about psychology, they always think of criminal profiling.

If you watch a TV programme or movie about psychology, there is always a criminal profiler who can make amazing predictions based on tiny amounts of data.

This is all a lie.

I wasn't going to be that blunt in the introduction but if you love criminal profiling and you want to be an FBI profiler in your career. Please do not read this book. This book will only tell you what the research says about profiling and how good or bad it is.

If you want a book that will say profiling is the most amazing thing ever and it's perfect. Please read another book.

However, if you want a book that explains what profiling is, how FBI profiling actually works and how useful it is in the real world and more. Then this IS the book for you.

Who Is This Book For?

If you're a psychology student, a trained psychologist professional or a person interested in forensic psychology. This is the book for you.

If you want a great engaging book that explains profiling in an easy-to-understand way. Then you will enjoy this book.

Also, this book is popular with people who want to learn more about profiling. Since this book isn't a hyped up book on profiling like so many others. And this book doesn't feed into the stereotypical profiling you see on TV, movies or in fiction books.

This is an engaging, conversational book on what are the two types of profiling, how effective are they and much more.

Who Am I?

I always like to know who the book is by that I'm reading because I like the book is written by a person who knows what they're talking about.

In case, you'll like me, I'm Connor Whiteley, an author of 15 psychology books as of March 2021.

Also, I'm the host of the weekly The Psychology World Podcast available on all major podcast apps. Each week I discuss the latest psychology news and an interesting psychology topic.

Finally, I am a psychology student at the University of Kent, England and later in 2021, I'll be working with a group of university researchers on two research projects.

So, now the introduction is done, let's see what Profiling is really about…

PART ONE:
FBI PROFILING

1.1- INTRODUCTION TO FBI PROFILING

Welcome to the first type of profiling, we'll be looking at in the book. This is the style of profiling that has been adorned and made famous by Hollywood, TV and movies all over the world.

However, like most things in TV and movies they get it wrong. So, let's look at what real FBI profiling is like.

Overall, profiling as practised by the FBI has failed to convince many psychologists of its effectiveness and this is the focus of the book, or at least this first part.

Generally, profiling is about predicting the characteristics of offenders.

I think this sounds great because it would be useful to know what characteristics the police need to look for. Since this would save the police time, money, and resources. Yet the truth is far from that simple.

Profiling as A Broad Term:

If I asked you 'What is Profiling?' what would you say?

Chances are you would say it's what they do on TV. And you would be right and wrong.

Due to a lot of profilers don't understand the board term of 'profiling'. This is only reinforced by Horant and Kennedy (1998) who defined the following 3 types of profiles and these should be carefully separated.

Firstly, you have what's known as crime scene profiling. This is where profilers use information from the crime scene to create a full picture of the unknown offender. Like, physical evidence.

Secondly, you have offender profiling. This is probably the type of profiling you see on TV and in movies. Where the profilers use a collection of empirical data to collate a picture of the characteristics of the offenders in a particular type of crime.

The final type of profiling is what's known as psychological profiling. I know a lot of people think this is the only think psychology does, but it isn't.

Since this is a type of profiling where profilers use standard personality questionnaires and interviews to determine if the person matches the known personality of a certain type of offender.

Therefore, there is absolutely no surprise that there's confusion about 'profiling'. Especially, when we consider how board profiling can be.

Viewpoints in Profiling:

As I write this book and I'm only on the third page, I had no idea I was going to be this passionate about the topic. But I might as well continue.

So, in profiling, there are two opposing viewpoints about what profiling should be. The first viewpoint is profiling is akin to clinical judgement which is informed by research but ultimately subjective. Due to the psychologist uses their expert opinion and the data to create the profile. This is what the FBI style of profiling uses.

Although, I need to say because my main background is in clinical psychology. There is a massive difference between clinical judgement and profiling. In clinical judgement, a psychotherapist uses a strong research base to inform their decisions. And as we'll see later in the book, FBI profiling could be considered lacking in its research base.

In addition, in an area in clinical psychology

called: Formulation. A psychotherapist would work with a client to create the clinical judgement. That's the simplified version because the client (mental health sufferer) brings the expertise in themselves. Whereas in FBI profiling you cannot work with an offender to create their profile because you often don't know who the offender is.

The other viewpoint is profiling must be informed by research and must be objective. This is a very important viewpoint for later in the book.

In the book, we'll look at both of these approaches to get a full picture of profiling.

Misconceptions and Profiling in Courts:

I know I've mentioned it already but there are so many misconceptions about profiling in TV, books, media and films.

As a result, some of these portray profilers as amazing people who can get great insights from small amounts of data.

In reality, they can't.

Whilst other media portrays profilers as flawed individuals.

However, something else these types of media teaches us is the importance of profiles to the criminal justice system all over the world. Yet in many countries, including the USA, profiling isn't particularly allowed in court unless you can prove it's based on data and not subjective opinions. Even then courts aren't too enthusiastic about profiles.

Bringing us back to the question of profiling's effectiveness in the real world.

Origins of profiling:

Like most things, there is an interesting backstory to profiling because Canter (2004) suggested profiling probably started in 1888 when doctor Thomas Bond created something akin to a profile of Jack the Ripper.

Also, for our non-British readers, Jack The Ripper was a major serial killer in the 1800s who was known for killing women. As well as he was never caught so there was a range of theories about who the killer was.

Going back to the story, when Thomas Bond said Jack the Ripper was probably a man of physical strength, great coolness and daring but without regular work.

Although, the origins of modern profiling can be traced back to 1956 and the work of the psychiatrist James A. Brussel on the New York bomber crimes. When Brussel used psychoanalysis to study the crime scene.

Then based on his assessment he said the offender was probably a middle-aged single male who lived with their sibling.

Interestingly, this turned out to be a somewhat accurate depiction of the offender George Metesky who committed the crimes.

Whilst Brussels had shown the power of the psychological approach to detective work. The profile wasn't the reason for the arrest. Yet it still shows how psychology can be useful.

Subsequently, one of Brussels's students, Howard Teten, became the first chief of the FBI Training Division at Quantico and housed in a nuclear bunker was the behavioural science unit. Then in the 1970s, they started to research the personalities, motivations and crimes of serial killers. Showing the sexual aspects in their crimes.

(I do understand if you're slightly confused since not all serial killer crimes are sexual in nature.)

This formed the research base for the FBI style of profiling. (Douglas, Brugess, Burgess and Ressler, 1992)

The Term 'Serial Killer'

Additionally, this FBI team created the term serial killer.

However, the idea of serial killers only committing crime sexual in nature is doubtful since there may be serial killers who don't show sexual elements in their crimes.

This doubt could be increased by the disagreement over the definition of a serial killer. Since the FBI says is a serial killer is a person who commits at least three murders over more than a month with an emotional cooling-off period in between.

Yet some people disagree. The disagreement is understandable because you could argue a hitman or women isn't a serial killer. Because they kill on the orders of other people.

Also, Ferguson, White, Stacey, Locen and Bhianai (2003) argued the lack of agreement in the definition of a serial killer makes it difficult for the field to progress.

As well as they reject Douglas et al (1992)'s idea that serial killers seek to express a need for power. Since it could be argued all criminals seek to express power.

Instead, they say sexual serial killers find killing pleasurable, kill 3 or more times and murders aren't under the direction of anyone else.

How would you define a serial killer?

1.2- THE PROCESS OF FBI PROFILING, THEIR METHODOLOGY AND THE PROCESS OF POLICE INVESTIGATIONS

FBI Profiling Process:

Moving onto how the FBI creates a profile, this involves a sequence of stages.

Stage 1:

Firstly, you have the data assimilation stage where the profiler collects data. For example, physical evidence and the corner's report.

Yet other less concrete material could still be vital to the ultimate profile of the offender. Like, the time of death could be key to the psychology of the offender.

This process is about gathering data about the personality of the offender. As well as the characteristic way the criminal works. The idea of the characteristic way is called the 'psychological signature' Which can be gleaned from the crime scene about the personality of the offence.

Although, the term personality is wrong here which is why the term characteristics replaces it in much of the modern literature.

Stage 2:

Afterwards, you have the crime scene classification stage where the profiler must decide the dichotomy of the 2 types of crime scene. Like, is this crime scene organised (showing it's a planned crime) or a disorganised crime scene?

A disorganised crime scene shows the crime wasn't planned. Equally, the crime scene could be mixed with elements of an organised and disorganised crime scene. As well as the thinking being a mixed crime scene tends to be a planned crime that goes wrong.

These types of crime scenes were based on early research by profilers. (Douglas et al, 1992) And early research could reliably classify a crime scene. (Ressler and Burgess, 1985)

Nevertheless, this is never the whole story. Since the same study found whilst on average 75% of profilers reached an agreement on the type of crime scene. There was drastic variation between the profilers and some profilers made a very different assessment of the sort of crime scene involved.

So, surely if profiling was as accurate as all these profiling superstars claim these results shouldn't happen?

Furthermore, the two types of crime scenes reveal different things about the psychology of the offenders. Like, according to Geberth (1996), the organised offender is classed as following the news media, alcohol is associated with crime, has a decent car, father had steady employment, offenders control mood during the crime and experienced inconsistent childhood discipline. Whereas the unorganised crime scene and the offender shows the opposite.

I understand the logic behind most of the above claims. But how does following the news make you more organised? It certainly makes you more informed, but I know a person who always watches the news. But organised is the last thing I would call them!

Stage 3

The third stage is the crime scene reconstruction stage. Since the crime scene is not a simple fixed event. It involves a complex set of circumstances. That can't be understood unless attempts are made to understand the events as a dynamic process between a minimum of 2 people.

Meaning the information collected in stage 1 is essential to the reconstruction where the profile retells what happened during the crime.

Although, the reconstruction doesn't have to recreate the event. Due to its purpose might be to clarify the offender's modus operandi, the reason for their offending. Knowing this could connect crimes to others.

Stage 4

The last stage is called the profile generation stage where the hypotheses about the offender are drawn together. This profile can include psychological factors, but the contents doesn't have to necessarily be psychological in nature.

As a result, it can include notes about behavioural habits, lifestyle, demographics and personality dynamics.

Function of the Profile

In FBI profiling, the profile may serve several functions. For instance, the profile can increase the efficiency of information processing by suggesting features of offending. This may help answer questions of links between a series of crimes and the possible number of different offenders involved.

Methodology of FBI profilers:

When it comes to the methods used by the FBI profilers, I have to say from a scientific standpoint, the original methods used to profile serial killers were far from rigorous. By today's standards, you would be laughed at most probably and you would never get them published in an academic journal.

As a result of the methods used originally had little formal research methodology and they consisted of little more than ad hoc interviews. (Canter, Alison, Alison and Wentink, 2004) This is where you have your data, and you try to make sense of it after collection. Which is different from the typical research process where you have your research hypothesis and empirically test it.

In addition, the data from these interviews were added to the subjective experience of the team.

In my opinion, this is rather horrifying because these team members might have years of experience dealing with serial killers. But can you honestly expect these team members to know every type of serial killer all over the USA, let alone the world?

Building upon this further, this methodology

(if you can call it that) has been publicised by many ex-profilers as a 'special art' (Canter, 2004) rather than a scientific endeavour.

Again, only reinforcing the lack of empirical rigour behind profiling.

If you're disheartened by the lack of scientific rigour in this area. Then you need to see the dedicated chapter to what research says on FBI profiling.

What Are the Main Features of An FBI Profile?

In a few chapters, I'll show you a real FBI profile but FBI profiles tend to be made up of a willingness to encompass a profiler's intuition or gut feeling as a component of profiles. As well as it features a relatively weak empirical database. This is small compared to the extent the method is used. Meaning you would have thought considering how often profiling is used, there would be more research data to support its claims.

Moreover, there is a concentration on the more serious, bizarre and extreme crimes. And a tendency to involve an extensive contact with the investigating team of police officers at all levels of the investigation and not simply creating a profile. Again, this only adds more subjective experiences and opinions of the officers.

This is disheartening to hear I think because

the rest of psychology, especially Social Psychology, teaches us how bad people can be at understanding others and how the social world works.

What Types of Crimes Get Profiled?

When I first entered the exciting world of researching profiling for this book, I thought lots of crimes could be profiled. Especially, before I learnt how extensive its limitations can be. So, I thought burglaries, murders, kidnapping and more could be profiled.

Sadly, that isn't necessarily true.

As a result, the types of crimes likely to be profiled is based on:

- Is it a bizarre or important crime? Since there's unfortunately little point profiling trivial crime. Because by its very nature, it's unlikely to be actively investigated.
- Does the crime show distinguishing characteristics at the scene? If it doesn't then it's a poor candidate for profiling.
- Is the profile analysis appropriate? This only tends to be the case if the crime scene indicates pathological psychological features. Like, taking a trophy.

Despite all this, profiling has been extended to

a much wider variety of types of crimes than the FBI profilers ever considered.

Process of Police Investigations:

We need to look at this area because profiling is adjunct to the police investigation.

Therefore, Innes (2002) conducted an extremely long and detailed study and I'm going to give you the summarised version.

The researcher found over 90% of English homicide cases are solved with it not being surprising that most crimes are done by an associate of the victim.

In addition, there is an information distinction between homicides with crimes being self-solvers and whodunnit.

The study found that roughly 70% of crimes are self-solvers where a suspect emerges very quickly due to a witness, evidence or an offender turns themselves in.

Typically, these self-solving cases involve the collection and analyses of information from the crime scene. Followed by the police pursuing various lines of inquiry.

Before concluding in the case construction stage. This involves, the selecting and organising the material into the account of events needed by the legal setting and this needs to be presented in the appropriate legal language. As explained in Forensic Psychology.

Whereas a whodunnit crime involves the initial response from the police. This is where the police deal with the available evidence at the crime scene. Followed by the police interviewing witnesses and a systematic search of the crime scene for physical evidence.

The next stage is the information burst where the police quickly generate large amounts of information from various sources. Here a number of suspects might be arrested and released without charge on the basis of having committed similar crimes in the past.

Afterwards, there's the suspect development stage where the police proceed to elicit more detail about possible suspects. As well as some suspects are dropped at this stage of the investigation.

Leading to other suspects becoming more suspicious as the evidence becomes clearer, and a prime suspect is being sought even on the basis of hunches.

Penultimately, there's the suspect targeting stage. This is where suspects are dropped and/or a prime suspect is revealed. The police change their approach to target this suspect with their information gathering effort.

Finally, you can have the case construction stage as before.

Linking this to profiling, it tends to be the whodunnit crimes that attract profiling.

1.3- FBI PROFILE EXAMPLE

After looking at FBI profiling more generally, I thought it would be good to look at a real FBI profile. Therefore, whilst this is shortened because the real profile is extremely long and as you'll see in a later chapter, most profiles contain minimal information. I hope this is still interesting.

Note: if anyone is offended by graphic details or certain types of crime, please skip the rest of this chapter.

This profile was used by Ressler, Burgess and Buglas (1988) in their study and in summary, the crime involved a nude 26-year-old lady who weighted 90 pounds was found dead. She wasn't dating men and her nipples were removed and placed on her body. As well as her face was severely beaten and... a pen and umbrella were inserted into her lady parts.

Well, that wasn't the most pleasant of crimes, but I think this goes to show profiling is *best* for crimes that are unusual.

As a result, the profile developed for this crime can be shortened to describe the following offender.

The offender is a white man between the ages of 25-35 years old, similar age to the victim, and drugs as well as alcohol were not material factors in this crime. This man was never married with average intelligence, but he dropped out of education.

In terms of employment, the man works in a skilled or unskilled occupation.

Personally, I think this profile is rather interesting. However, I cannot for the life of me figure out how the skilled or unskilled occupation is useful. Because I cannot see how that narrows down the offender's potential job. Can you?

Anyway, when it came to the generation of this profile, the profilers used a few threads of thinking using the available information.

For example, the thought the killer tends to be of a similar age and race to the victim. As well as the killer's fantasies are important in such extreme cases. With this fantasy perhaps being used as a blueprint or plan for the crime. Therefore, the characteristics of the fantasy can be seen in the contents of the crime.

Additionally, there's little evidence of preparedness in the crime except in the killer's fantasy.

Clearly, this crime is sexual in nature, but the offender uses substitutes for penetration. Suggesting the offender has a lack of experience or inadequateness. (I suppose this is logical?)

Finally, the offender defecated at the crime scene. Suggesting the sexual nature, the killing and the other components of the crime took a long time. As well as the murder happened in an exposed area, increasing the risk of getting caught. Therefore, suggesting the offender was familiar with the location.

After the profile was given to the police, it led to a prime suspect. This was a man whose father lived in the building. He was convicted based on the bite marks that matched his dental patterns.

Thinking About the Profile:

So, I will give credit where it's due, the profile and the threads of thought did predict it was a man, but I think we can agree it's uncommon for a woman to sexually attack a woman.

Also, I can fully understand the idea of fantasy in the crime because otherwise, I can't see how a person could think or want to do that to someone else.

Nevertheless, I want to point out the profile might have led to a suspect, but it wasn't a part of the basis of the conviction. So, again this raises the question of: how useful are profiles in the criminal justice system?

1.4 WHAT RESEARCH SAYS ABOUT PROFILING?

This has to be one of my favourite chapters because in the next couple of chapters, I'm going to be explaining the research support, if you can call it that, for profiling.

If you think profiling is the gold standard of psychology, then please do not read this chapter. It will probably break your heart. But I do love this chapter.

So, let's crack on!

Generally, profiles lack justifications for their claims and assertions they make about the offender. Since Alison, Smith and Morgan (2003) and Alison, Smith, Eastran and Rainbow (2002) studied a selection of US and UK profiles. They coded and analysed 3090 statements. The vast majorities of these statements were facts already known to the police, about the profiler's competence or gave warning about the profile's limitation.

Out of this only, 28% of the profile contained information about the offender.

Even out of this 28%, most of these statements were unsubstantiated claims. With only 16% of the statements being provided with some justification. As well as 1% of the statements were simply illogical.

Additionally, Wilson, Lincoln and Kocsis (1999) suggested that anecdotes of profiling's success are what dominates assessment about its validity.

So, where do I begin to explain the problems?

Personally, I cannot understand why profiling is meant to be so great if only 28% of the profile actually contains information.

That would be like me spending the majority of this book explaining why I'm qualified to write the book and be telling you about myself.

I would hate that; you would hate that.

Additionally, referring back to psychology as a science. I don't understand why the profilers can't justify their statements. This is my main problem with profiling and how the media, TV and movies portray profiling. My problem is because of profiling being what everyone thinks psychology is and profiling is not scientific. This is why a lot of people think psychology is a fake science. At least in my experience.

Plus, it doesn't help that because of profiling I had to constantly prove to my family and friends that psychology was a science and not profiling.

Does Profiling Work?

In all honesty, it doesn't matter what I say or what the rest of forensic psychology says about profiling. Since the main issue is *how effective is profiling?* This is vitally important.

To argue about its effectiveness, Devery (2010) and a lot of other researchers have strongly argued that profiling has never shown itself to be devoted to scientific rigour.

He suggests there are few articles that show the scientific rigour of profiling and even these articles are overshadowed by popular upbeat books on profiling.

In addition, he describes profiling as a 'compendium of common-sense intuition' which can be put down to or simplified as 'educated guesses and wishful thinking'

I agree!

Additionally, Devery (2010) adds finding examples of profiling positively impacting a police investigation is hard. In fact, it's a lot more common to find examples of profilers impeding an investigation by sending the police in the wrong direction.

The exception to this seems to be Canter and Wentink's (2004) study of Holmes' and Holmes' (1998) classification of serial killers cases where they analysed serial killer cases. To give their system as much chance of success as possible the researchers coded each of Holmes' and Holmes' 5 types of characteristics.

The types of killers are as followed:

- Visionary killers- these killers are largely acting on the orders from voices or visions from God, angels, demons and the like.
- Mission killers- here the killers decide to target groups or a type of people because they believe the world would be better off without them.
- Lust killers- part of the killing is the fulfilment of sexual fantasies. Sex is the process of enjoyment.
- Thrill killers- these killers enjoy the process of killing by getting pleasure and excitement from it.

- Power/ control killers- in this group the gratification comes from the fact they have control over the victim. As well as the dominance over the other person is the motive. Also, in this group, the killer's pleasure is maximum by extending the killing over time.

Furthermore, Canter and Wentzel (2004) claimed their study provided limited support for these typologies. Yet simple direct support for these typologies categories didn't emerge in the data.

Again, another study showing the lack of research support for profiling.

To summarise their findings the idea of there being a power/ control group of killers is flawed because these characteristics were very typical of the entire sample and didn't form their own distinctive group.

Additionally, whilst there did seem to be a group of thrill-seeking variables. This was largely considered to be down to the restrictive nature of the killing methods used. Like, gagging.

However, other characteristics of the group according to Holmes and Holmes didn't emerge clearly. Like, the weapon being missing. Suggesting these characteristics are part of other patterns.

Nonetheless, there seemed to be some support for visionary killers because the characteristic behaviours of this group did co-occur at crime scenes. Like, bludgeoning the victim to death. Also, some of the key characteristics, like leaving the weapon in the victim, didn't come from this group. Also, facial disfigurement was close to the core of this group. Whereas Holmes and Holmes claimed in was apart of the lust killer group.

Overall, these findings show that even simple typologies lack sufficient support to be used without adapting these typologies first.

I would have quite liked this idea to have research support because I can think of a few uses of knowing the types of killers and the typical characteristics of them. However, in the real world there just isn't enough consistency or research to be able to reliably group offenders into types.

Furthermore, Canter and his co-workers ran a statistical analysis to determine if the idea of organised and disorganised crime scenes did predict the different traits of the offenders as the FBI profilers believed. The results found an organised crime scene and a disorganised crime scene didn't show their unique characteristics distinctively. There was a subgroup of organised characteristics that did correspond to the organised crime scene. Yet that's mainly down to most serial killers being organised.

And not being a unique group to themselves.

On the whole, there is minimal research support for even the basic FBI profiling principles. Considering everything in FBI profiling is built upon this crime scene distinction. I cannot see how anyone can claim that FBI profiling is scientific at all.

Anyway, to end this damning chapter, I should mention despite its supposed (yes, I can be diplomatic) less scientific rigour, the FBI approach to profiling has been subjected to more validity assessment than the statistical profiling we'll look at next.

Saying of next, I wonder what the police and psychologists think about profiling?

1.5 WHAT DO THE POLICE AND PSYCHOLOGISTS THINK ABOUT PROFILING?

Continuing our look at the effectiveness of FBI profiling, we need to look at the opinions of the police and psychologists. Since it is these professionals that use the profile in everyday life.

Consequently, a strange finding has been the police say profiling is useful but it doesn't lead to an arrest.

Again, I don't particularly understand this point because if the profile doesn't lead to the arrest. How do the police know it's useful?

On a minor side note, this is a very interesting area of forensic psychology because it's always interesting to see what 'lay' people think about certain areas of the Criminal Justice System. If you want to know how people's opinions and beliefs affect the

Justice System, definitely check out Forensic Psychology.

Returning back to the theory, Alison, Smith and Morgan (2003) got a real FBI profile and asked police officers about the known factors of the case and the person convicted of the case.

In the case used the criminal was a 19 years old unemployed actor who was a stranger to the victim. As well as he had no relationships in his life nor any abuse in the family and he attempted suicide.

The real FBI profile can be summarised to say the offender was a white man who was between the ages of 25 to 35 years old of average intelligence but a university or high school dropout. Also, he didn't want the woman to scream for help.

Additionally, he was probably a very confused person, possibly with previous mental conditions. He had a pornography collection with no military history and may be unemployed.

On the whole, the profile was very good because it did correctly guess the age, race, employment status. I'm not sure how they got the pornography collection part or if it's that significant.

In terms of the police, the police officers overwhelming said the profile was useful to their investigation. Whereas the forensic professionals were less enthusiastic.

Amazingly, the study went even further and showed a similar group of officers a made up offender. Who was an abusive 37-year-old and had several relationships with women.

What's amazing is these officers claimed the profile was just as useful in this case than the profile with the real offender. Despite, these two profiles being polar opposites. Therefore, showing the accuracy of the profile doesn't impact how useful the officers think it is!

Overall, making police officers not a good judge of its effectiveness.

What Psychologists Think About Profiling:

When I first had my forensic psychology module at university, my lecture made sure we knew within the first five minutes of the lecture that forensic psychology is a great area. And forensic psychology wasn't profiling, and he basically said profiling isn't worth the paper it's written on.

Now, I'm not that extreme in my opinion but for a highly respected forensic psychologist to say that... it had to be true. At least to some extent.

Generally speaking, FBI profiling is treated with scepticism by psychologists and other people.

These other people tend to be the general public.

In an effort to research this, Jones, Boccaccini ad Miller (2006) survey psychologists and psychiatrists. Their results found 95% of psychiatrists and 85% of psychologist thought profiling was a useful tool of law enforcement.

However, doubts were raised about its scientific basis. Due to over 97% of surveyed people thought profiling needs empirical research to support it. Whereas a tiny, tiny minority of less than 3% thought profiling was scientifically reliable.

Interestingly, only 25% of them felt knowledgeable about profiling.

Even accounting for the perceived lack of knowledge the surveyed people had on profiling. That's still an extremely high number of people who do not believe profiling is scientifically reliable.

Do Professionals Produce Better Profiles Than Lay People?

There is some evidence that professionals produce more detailed and informative reports that contain more predictions than non-experts. Like, a comparison group of students as used in Kocsis (2003) and Kocsis, Middledrop and Try (2005)

Furthermore, there are additional studies that

support this conclusion. Like, Piniznotto and Finkel (1999)

Yet these results are hardly controversial and there are some methodology limitations. Making the findings only partially convincing. For example, the situation in which the profiles are produced as somewhat artificial as the non-experts complete a checklist rather than creating the profile themselves.

Meaning I suppose you can outright say profilers make better profiles than lay people. But due to the methodological issues, I doubt you can convincingly say this.

Additionally, while these studies show profiles are overall more accurate than non-profilers. their superiority can be questioned due to the lack of consistency in all areas of profiling.

For instance, there's little difference between non-profilers and profilers in regard to the quality of their predictions about offender behaviour.

Wait a minute, isn't that the entire point of profiling?

Aren't profilers meant to produce insightful predictions better than lay people?

However, this is an extremely complex issue because then you have the issue of what is an expert?

(Kocsis, 2010)

A formally trained person?

An officer who provides profiles to courts but has no formal training?

Then you have researchers making radically different claims, but their datasets use the same studies or mostly. Like, Kocsis (2003) and Snook et al (2010).

Therefore, you cannot simply say one approach is better than the other. These factors partially explain some of the disagreement between researchers who look at essentially much of the same data. I recommend looking at Kocsis (2013) for a more detailed summary of the argument.

I think we have to admit it is strange that profilers get such radically different predictions from effectively the same data. Again though, I think this highlights the non-scientific underpinnings of FBI profiling. Since you wouldn't get radically different predictions from the next style of profiling we'll look at. Or from statistical analysis done in SPSS.

Whilst we're evaluating the FBI style of profiling, we need to look at their theoretical underpinning. So we know the assumptions of FBI profiling are there are characteristics of the offender that are represented at the crime scene, crime scenes can be efficiently categorised and an offender's crime can show characteristic patterns.

One way to evaluate and explain these assumptions are what been termed the Homology Hypothesis. Or in friendly terms, this means that the characteristics of the crime scene and the characteristics of the offender converge.

In addition, Snook, Cullen, Dennell, Taylor and Gendreau (2008) argue that the typologies used in profiling don't have any real substance in the empirical literature. The example they pointed to was the organised/ disorganised crime scene typology that, as we saw earlier, has no research support from the little research that has been conducted so far.

Additionally, Snook et al (2008) argue it's an innate problem that the FBI approach to profiling is based on trait approaches in personality. When modern ideas in psychology realised that situational factors are more likely to drive behaviour than if someone has a particular personality trait.

I cannot begin to explain how this idea of certain personality traits being used in FBI profiling is technically wrong. But there's a chapter on this towards the end.

For the homology hypothesis to work or be remotely 'true' offenders need to show constancy in terms of their offending style over the course of a number of offences.

In reality, this doesn't often happen because the offender learns by experience and learn what does and doesn't work. This may lead to the abandonment of ineffective strategies whilst keeping and reinforcing effective strategies. Suggesting how difficult this idea of consistency is in the real world.

Now, we've thoroughly examined the FBI approach to profiling. Let's look at the other more scientific approach to profiling.

PART TWO: STATISTICAL PROFILING

2.1- INVESTIGATIVE PSYCHOLOGY AND STATISTICAL AND GEOGRAPHICAL PROFILING

The other approach to profiling follows the viewpoint that profiling should be subjective and supported by research. I do prefer this approach a lot more because it shows psychology as a strong practical science. And I really hope you enjoy this type of profiling as much as I do.

This approach to profiling is called Statistical and Geographical Profiling.

David Canter:

Before he worked in investigative psychology, the social psychologist David Canter worked in a developing area of psychology, called environmental psychology. This area seeks to understand the interaction between people and the environment they live in.

Therefore, David Canter used some of the basic assumptions of environmental psychology to form his distinctive approach to profiling.

In the 1980s he met with senior police management to talk about using psychology to aid police work (Canter, 1994) and he quickly became intrigued by a string of unsolved rapes in London. Now known to have been committed by John Duffy either alone or with David Mulcaly.

During the investigation, Canter created the first-ever profile in the UK by incorporating qualitative data into his analysis. As well as he drew on simple information like: maps showing where the crimes happened and chronologies (time) of when the offences took place.

Following this Canter faced a list of rapes possibly done by the same or different offenders. Leading him to code and analysis each rape's characteristics. Allowing him to group the rapes with similar characteristics together to be done by the same person. Like, the offender tying the victim's thumb behind their back.

In the end, Canter's profile included 17 different elements, most of them turning out to be correct. Here's a sample of the profile:

"Possibly arrested some time after 24th

October 1983. Probably semi-skilled or skilled job, involving weekend work or caused labour from June 1984 onwards," (Canter, 1994, p.39)

My favourite part of this process has to be he managed to give specific details by superimposing maps of successive years of offences on top of each other.

In other words, he laid maps detailing the year and time and the location of the rape on top of one another. Allowing him to see patterns and trends in the maps.

Therefore, he could see there was no offending at certain times. Suggesting a possible arrest. Also, there were no changes in the geographical locations of the crimes suggesting the offender hadn't moved.

Overall, Canter concluded the locations of the other first offences mentioned in his profile confirmed were the offender lived.

Interestingly, John Duffy was at the bottom of the police's list of suspects but shortly after Canter discussed the profile with the police. John Duffy was arrested. His co-offender wasn't found until years later when Duffy finally revealed is identity.

Focusing more on the approach itself, features of Canter's approach can be seen early on.

Like, his focus on empirical evidence to back up the profile and his search for patterns.

Interestingly, in recent times, some people prefer to change the term *offender profiling* for the border term *Behavioural Investigative Advice* (BIA). This is how psychologists, particularly in the UK, give their evidence-based advice to the police. (Alison, Goodwill, Almond, Van Den Heuuel and Winter, 2010)

2.2- GEOGRAPHICAL PROFILING

Continuing our look at Canter's approach to profiling, he placed an interesting emphasis on geographical profiling. You can think of this as a sub-feature of statistical profiling.

Therefore, Canter's early work involved a form of geographical profiling and criminologists have long known the importance of environmental factors in crime. For instance, the Chicago school of sociology (Shaw and McKay, 1942) found offenders tend to be concentrated in particular parts of a city.

Subsequently, you have Routine Activation Theory as well. This theory is outlined in My Forensic Psychology of Theft and Property Crime book. But in short, this theory proposes that it is the structure and activities of their everyday crimes that provides them with the opportunity to commit crime.

Origins of Geographical Profiling

Whilst people are unsure of when geographical profiling was first used. Some people think it could be in 1980 in the UK Yorkshire Ripper murders. Due to, in this case, the centre of distribution for the murders was found to be the city of Bradford. This was revealed to be where the Ripper lived.

Other people believe geographical profiling was invented by detective Rossono of the Vancouver Police Department in Canada. Rossono (2000) summarised his early findings as criminals tend to offend close to their homes and there is a decline in offences further away from home. As well as the precise patterns depend on the crime. For example, if we take burglary it's *better* to rob a rich city centre than a neighbour sometimes.

Linking to Psychology:

The psychological approach to geographical profiling would seek to examine the associations between psychological factors and crime geography.

To test this idea, Snook, Cullen, Makros and Harboorts (2003) studied how 53 German serial killers made their decisions about killing locations. The researchers found the chosen location was mediated by economic, social and cognitive characteristics. Like, younger killers tended to stay closer to home whilst high IQ killers tended to travel further.

In addition, people with their own transport tended to travel further. This makes sense obviously because I cannot see someone wanting to travel back home after killing someone on the train.

Consequently, this study amongst others shows there's a link between crime and spatial factors in the literature. Yet are crimes committed by the same offender similar geographically?

On the whole, there is some support for this because Dennel and Canter (2002) found there is a degree of stability to the offender's characteristic location for their crimes. In other words, offenders tend to choose locations with similar characteristics. Like, a quiet suburban area.

Although, great care needs to be taken when setting the decision point which differentiates the likely linked crimes from the unlikely linked ones.

In much simpler terms, when deciding the size of the circle that you create, the idea being all the linked crimes are inside the circle. You need to be careful not to make the circle too small because you'll miss other crimes by the same offender. Equally, you don't want to make the circle too big as this increases the likelihood of you picking crimes that you think are linked but they were committed by a different offender.

According to Haginoya (2014), there are two ways to predict where the offender lives in relation to the crime scenes.

Firstly, there's Canter's Circle Hypothesis as proposed by Canter and Gregory (1994). This works by finding the two furthest crime scenes and drawing a circle around each crime scene. Then the idea is at the two points where these two circles meet, you draw a line. With this line's point being the centre. All of the other crimes should be inside.

Another way is the suspicious area model. (Mimoto and Fukada, 1999) This method assumes the offender's home is the point where the shortest sums of the distances to each crime scene.

Subsequently, the average distance from this point is used as a radius for the circle where the offender is believed to live.

Despite this method giving a smaller search area than Canter's way. Hammond (2014) warns that rather different parameters might be needed when geographical profiling is used in other locations where it wasn't developed. Like, suburban or rural areas. Since these areas are considerably more spread out than city areas.

Also, it's worth noting the term Marauder is used to describe an offender living inside the circle. Whereas an offender who lives outside the circle is called a Commuter.

Like everything in psychology and statistics, geographical profiling needs to be optimised. So, to optimise the decision criterion, you need to use the Receiver Operating Characteristics or ROC curve. This is used to make a binary decision. Such as, to determine if the crimes area is linked or not.

In simpler terms, it's a graph of the true positive and false positives for the different values of the decision criterion.

The ideal decision rule is about maximizing the true positives, the correctly identified linked crimes, and minimizing the false positives. The crimes identified as linked but they aren't.

An Interesting Use and Wrap Up

An interesting use of geographical profiling was in Southern Sweden where it was used to determine the location of an obscene telephone caller who was calling children. Dragnet, the geographical profiling program, managed to identify the very precise area where the offender lived. (Ebberline, 2008)

Overall, geographical profiling works on the assumption that the offender's decision about where to commit the crime isn't a random process.

However, geographical profiling doesn't tell us where the offender will strike next spatially. Johnson (2014) highlighted crime locations are like animal foraging in principle. As a result of animals go out from a central point and hunt outwards until they find food. An interesting way of looking at geographical. If not a little weird!

2.3- THE RESEARCH BASE OF PROFILING

The next part of this book is going to focus more on profiling as a whole instead of exclusively looking at FBI and Statistical Profiling. Although, this part of the book will slightly lean towards statistical profiling because there are more research points, we need to look at.

The research Base Approach to Criminal Profiling:

One of Canter's main insights was the lack of research into the interactions between offenders and their real-life environment. Compared to the mass of literature on offenders after they had been arrested.

I do agree because this is one problem with forensic psychology is a lot of the research sample is biased toward arrested criminals. Compared to the criminals that don't get arrested. There ways around this as shown in Forensic Psychology but it isn't perfect.

As shown earlier, the fact that Canter had focused on the literature and empirical-based method has served him well in investigating the railway rapes.

After investigating the railway rapes, he started to systematically study the behavioural characteristics of offences. Similar to FBI profiling, Canter believed the crime scene contained important features. Showing features of the offender's behaviour that can be used to distinguish them.

The main difference between FBI and statistical profiling is statistical profiling focuses on establishing an empirical relationship using statistical techniques in large data sets. This is also known as real science and scientific rigour!

Which as we know compared to the FBI style that is considered weak in terms of its empirical core.

Furthermore, statistical profiling is based on its research-oriented ethos without relying on clinical insight and intuition.

I think this is why I prefer this approach to profiling because it is based on the scientific method and it doesn't rely on a person's subjective opinions. Do not get me wrong, I know the value of subjective opinions when it comes to clinical psychology. But they have to be used correctly. Another reason why I love the topic of Formulation in Psychotherapy.

Additionally, when it comes to the classification of the crime scene, Canter's statistical approach is empirically based since he uses specialised statistical methods. Like, the smallest space analysis. This is a statistical method that aims to identify how likely features of the crime scene are likely to exist or coexist with another feature.

For example, there are some features in rape that are quite common. Like virginal penetration is almost universal in female rapes and others that aren't as common. For example, cunnilingus.

Overall some of these behaviours frequently occur in rape and others are rarely found together.

House (1997)

Consequently, House (1997) analysed the co-occurrence as well as the frequency of certain rape behaviours. The statistical analysis showed a diagram of common and uncommon behaviour in rapes.

For example, vaginal penetration, clothing removal and elements of surprise are very close to the centre. Suggesting their commonality in rapes where apologises, torture and theft are further away from the centre. Suggesting their rarity in rapes.

Moreover, rape characteristics that were close together in the diagram tend to occur together often. Despite them being uncommon overall. For example, the theft of money and theft of personal belonging were close together because they tend to co-occur frequently but they're rare overall.

In addition, the statistical analysis was organised into 4 major themes of rape. These could be considered types of rapists, but you need to be careful about calling it a typology. Due to the flaws and limitations of typologies. The statistical analysis included the themes of criminality, aggression, sadism and intimacy. These suggest there's a variety of mental scripts for carrying out the rape.

Interestingly, House's wok does have a practical application because the type of rape is associated with the offender's criminal history.

Another interesting feature is the statistical analysis revealed some patterns in these groups. Such as the sadistic group was less likely to have an arrest and conviction history. Whereas the criminality group were the most likely.

Also, the sadism and intimacy groups tended to be low on convictions for property crime. As well as the sadistic group were least likely to have convictions for violence compared to the other groups. Yet the sadism and intimacy groups were most likely to have convictions for deception.

This research could be used to find potential

suspects. If these suspects have 'good' criminal records with relevant information that is good quality.

Additionally, this would help police interviewing and record keeping become more effective. Despite the fact, this could never prove a person did the crime unless the police had the suspect's DNA on file, and a sample from the crime scene to compare it to.

What About Murder?

So far in the book, we've looked at research into lots of areas of crime. But what does research into murder characteristics say?

To find out Salfati and Canter (1998) studied the relationship between murder crime scenes and the murder's characteristics using 82 British murders where at the time of discovery the police didn't know who the offender who. Despite these murders being called the stranger murders by the police, 74% of these murders were committed by people at least slightly known to the victim. The data revealed 48 variables that fell broadly fell into these categories.

- Characteristics of the victim.
- Information that reflected characteristics of the offender.
- Actions or things done to the victim
- Traces of behaviour at the crime scene.

These categories lead to a lot of interesting information.

Information features of the crime including:

- 12% of the offenders served in the armed forces.
- 23% of offenders had previously been married.
- Only 12% of the murders involved sexual elements. This is interesting because it contradicts the beliefs of FBI profiling.
- 48% of murders were married and living with a partner
- 40% of offenders had previous convictions with theft being the most common at 22%, burglary at 18% and violence at 15%
- Most offenders were male at 72%
- 66% of the homicides happened in the evening.
- 76% of the murders didn't move the body to another location.
- 44% found in their own homes.
- Younger offenders had a mean age of 27 years old with a range of 15 to 29 years old.
- Lastly, unemployment was common amongst the killers at 41%.

As we can see there's a lot of good data to think about and this raises questions that are beyond the scope of this book. For example, how does unemployment link to murder?

Building upon this further, the study went further by using a smallest space analysis. The researchers found two-thirds of these murders can be placed into one of the three categories: instrumental opportunistic, instrumental cognitive and expressive impulsive.

Subsequently, each of these categories tended to be corresponded with particular offender characteristics. Like, expressive impulsive murders tend to have limbs attacked and single wounds at the crime scene don't by female offenders with various previous offences in short.

Then other third of murders fit into all three categories.

However, as impressive as this is, there are caveats. Like:

- How well can offender characteristics be predicted from crime scene characteristics?
- How useful is this in police work?
- What does this tell the police about where to search for the offender?
- If so, how effective would this search be?

Whilst we do not know the answers at the present time. It definitely makes for interesting points to think about.

These studies do raise the point though that there is potential for profiling and these categories to be used in the real world. However, without research showing the results of any direct input into police investigations. It is still difficult to state with any degree of certainty the effectiveness of any type of profiling.

Personally, I want to stress though statistical profiling, compared to FBI profiling, understand better that crime scene characteristics and offender characteristics are only probabilities and not certainties.

For example, at an instrumental cognitive crime scene, it is only probable that the offender has served a prison sentence or the armed forces.

2.4- THE HOMOLOGY ISSUE AND BASIC THEORY

The final massive issue we need to look at in profiling, before we look at a fun topic to wrap up the book, is the homology issue. Homology in profiling is the characteristics of the crime scene that can predict the characteristics of the offender.

Before we dive into the theory and memory, try taking a moment and thinking about it for yourself. What problems or issues do you think we could face with homology?

Whilst evidence of this Homology Hypothesis has been given in earlier chapters of the book. It must be said there is not an overwhelming amount of support for it nor can the hypothesis be dismissed.

Although, the idea of there being consistencies in offending can be found in a few ways. For example, the consistency or crime linkage is

1

built on the belief that there are consistencies in offending characteristics of a particular offender. Sometimes referred to as the Consistency Hypothesis. (Canter, 1994) This is the idea that offenders commit crimes in a consistent manner and this hypothesis is used to predict if different crime scenes are committed by the same offender.

Another concept that provides evidence for consistencies in offender characteristics is matching. Which is the idea that the crime scene characteristics match the typical characteristics of the offender that commits that sorts of crime. Like, the suggested negative relationship between the age of the sex attack victim and the age of the offender. Or another example is the stereotypical characteristics of a shoplifter is a teenage male.

The last concept providing some evidence for consistencies in offender characteristics is homology. With this type of consistency seeking the relationship between crime scene characteristics and the particular characteristics of the individual who committed the offence.

On the whole, I think we can agree there is pretty limited support for homology but there's still some support. Possibly meaning more research needs to be done to find more evidence or there's a weak relationship that we don't fully understand. For instance, why do some studies show evidence and not others? Could it be down to methodological issues? Sample Bias? Without more research, we might not know.

Consistency in Offending:

As Snook et al (2014) pointed out the evidence for these relationships is weak and the underlying assumption of FBI style profiling is invalid. So, a more appropriate conclusion for statistical profiling could be there is some tentative support for these relationships. Yet largely only at a modest level.

On the other hand, some studies do provide support for this as previously mentioned. Such as Yokota et al (2007) conducted a very long and detailed study using real criminal records and offences from the past and brand new cases. Then the researchers used a program to test the homology to find their computer profiling system showed great promise. Suggesting there to be good homology in the data. Then the study went even further by adding the geographical locations of the crimes as well as the lands of Japan. Resulting in the correct suspect being at the top of the list increasing to 56% of the time. Heavily implying there is a relationship between these characteristics.

Nonetheless, I certainly think Sorochinski and Salfati (2010) makes a great point when they conducted an analysis they termed the 'consistency of the inconsistencies' and the researchers found the research painted a wanted picture of the consistency in serial murder crime scenes.

Crime Linkage:

A few pages ago, I mentioned the term crime linkage, and this is concerned with the consistencies of behaviours from a crime scene and it turns out, this idea could be valid. Regardless of the validity of profiling.

Interestingly, Tonkin, Bond and Woodhams (2009) decided to test this using footprint analysis at a crime scene.

Now, this is a very clever way to test this since compared to profiling footprint analysis is a stalwart component of forensic science. But only 8% of crime scenes had good enough footprints to run the analysis. Then of this 8%, 40% of the footwear was identified.

Leading the researchers to apply profiling methods to 160 domestic burglaries, and they conducted an analysis of the footwear price. As well as they obtained background information about crimes from the police.

The really interesting part is there was a consistency between the offender's footwear characteristic and the crime. As a result of the researcher found linked crime scenes committed by the same offender. With the difference in footwear cost being quite small at £5 on average. Whereas the difference for unlinked crime scenes being much large at £16 on average.

Consequently, this provides evidence for the matching and similarity principles. Since the shoe cost is linked to deprivation and living conditions as well as employment status.

However, we sadly have to consider the reality we live in because interesting as this is, it probably doesn't provide enough criteria to narrow things down to help identify the offender.

Regardless of that tiny fact, I still think it's pretty amazing!

A final study that supports and slightly doesn't support crime linkage is Bouhara, Johnson and Porter (2016) who studied English burglaries and they found burglars use consistent behaviours in offending. Yet only some burglars used identifiable patterns of behaviour. Therefore, this results in only partial support for the specificity principle.

The main reason for this is because offender's change their behaviour over time and this reduces the consistency in their crime. For example, they may change their behaviour because the offenders change and develop new tactics and increase their efficiency over time. Including an increase in their confidence.

Additionally, the offender's goals may change. Leading to the offender changing their behaviour in order to meet these goals. Like, in sexual crimes the offender's fantasies may change.

Lastly, the victim's resistance or other situational factors could make the offender change their method or behaviour.

On the whole, after looking at the evidence, this is some support for homology and crime linkage. But there is still a lot of factors that can decrease the consistency in offender behaviour. Therefore, this does highlight the need for people, be it profilers or police, to be mindful about not being too restricted when deciding what crimes are related and the ones that aren't.

2.5- PERSONALITY AND PROFILING

To wrap up this book, I thought it would be interesting to look at personality because there's a massive misconception that criminals have a particular personality that makes them commit crime. So, I wonder how this misconception or area of psychology relates to profiling?

It all honesty, this is a very difficult area. Mainly due to how the FBI style of profiling has treated personality research, but traditionally and typically profiling poorly predicting personality characteristics.

Although, this may be down to the poor personalities theories it uses and the lack of research.

As a result, an examination of the research shows little criminal activity can be related to a normal personality theory. Suggesting forensic psychology needs its own personality model. This is missing from the literature. The closest research to a criminal personality model is Eysenck's Biosocial Theory that has a few references to personality. Yet this theory is way too board for profiling. And I mean this theory covers A LOT of ground!

As a result, Youngs (2004) decided to make an argument that offending and personality did link. Starting with the fact there has been little research done into the styles of offenders and personality. As well as most personality research uses clinical tools.

There is absolutely nothing wrong with this except it is possible these clinical tools are only useful in identifying clinical or abnormal traits, not criminal traits.

Resulting in Youngs arguing for researchers to consider circumstances in which there'll be a differentiating relationship between styles of offending and personality traits. He argued the research into offending styles must be empirically defeasible. In other words, scientific. Also, the conceptions of personality employed must be appropriate to criminal behaviour and not a normal concept from personality. As well as empirical research must be informed by an understanding of the way behaviour is shaped by personality.

I know this might have confused a few people because this sounds obvious. Since all psychology

8

research should use appropriate concepts and empirical research. Yet as Woodhams, Hollin and Bull (2007) argues forensic researchers are using approaches to personality that were abandoned decades ago by personality researchers. Thus, they need to adopt modern approaches to allow them to understand personality and the different crime scene behaviours in different offences.

The two fundamental aspects to this, for lack of a better term, modernisation of the research is the research must consider the consistency across an offender's successive crimes might not be the same, regardless of the behaviour in question. And the situation-dependent behaviours, of course, showed fewer consistencies overtime.

In addition, Woodhams et al argue research mustn't ignore the 'ifs' (situational factors) in the 'if-then' relationships. (Mischel, 1999) Where the 'thens' are the distinctive ways of behaving in offending.

Furthermore, Youngs (2004) suggested the fundamental Interpersonal Relations Orientation (FIRO) theory could be a means of assessing interpersonal interaction characteristics that could have a bearing on the offender's criminal style. (Shutz, 1994) Because an individual's interpersonal style, the way how they interact with other people, will be reflected in the characteristic behaviours they receive from others.

Overall, the theory has 3 main personality characteristics. The first is control. This is made up of two largely unrelated parts. Expressed control, which is the willingness to control others. Then you have received control. The willingness to be controlled by others. Oddly, people high in expressed control may be resistant to control OR be willing to be controlled by others.

The second characteristic is inclusion, and expressed inclusion is all about a person's desire to be included, belong and receive attention from others.

Finally, you have openness, and expressed openness refers to people who bond with others through emotions and closeness. These people tend not to be withdrawn or closed in their relationships.

Relating these personality characteristics to crime, a statistical analysis of young men aged 14 to 28 years old who completed a lengthy questionnaire demonstrated expressive behaviours were consistent with arson, sex in public and breaking into empty buildings to cause damage. Whereas expressed control was related to violence. Also, high scorers on received control had a tendency to commit property crime.

Overall, taken with other findings, this appears to support Youngs' argument for personality and offending.

CONCLUSION

To conclude this book, I have to admit this was great fun to write and explore this great topic with you. So, a massive thank you from me for joining me on this journey.

We'll definitely covered a lot of ground in the book from the unscientific and overly popular FBI style of profiling to the more empirical statistical profiling. We certainly learnt a lot together.

So, to conclude the book, I wanted to add there is some statistical evidence that different crime scene statistics might be associated with different offender characteristics.

However, this is not the same as stating criminal profiles lead to the identification of the offender or its operational usefulness.

On a personal note, before I started researching this book, I knew profiling wasn't that good or exciting. But I never expected profiling to be as divided and diverse with the two viewpoints as I discovered.

Would I ever become a profiler?

No.

No, I just wouldn't. For many reasons but the main reason is because psychology is a science and whilst even statistical profiling is scientific in nature. I would prefer to focus on mainstream psychology with mental health and clinical psychology. Yet I will always love forensic psychology.

Another reason is because of what Chifflet (2015) concluded "Assessing evidence of the validity of offender profiling does not yield an entire reassuring picture. There still appears to be fundamental gaps and shortcomings as a foundation for the discipline as well as in the research undertaken to validate and advance the framework. Furthermore, there is little empirical evidence to conclude unequivocally that profiling works in practice or that profilers offer significantly more accurate predictions than non-profilers this has undoubtedly led any many to wonder how the discipline succeeded in permeating criminal investigations and legal proceedings," (p.251)

I completely agree with that statement above

and I really hope there is more research done in the future to try and deal with these gaps in the literature.

Finally, whilst statistical profiling is the best option and the most research supported type of profiling. There is a lot of work that needs to be done if statistical profiling is ever going to be as influential as the FBI profilers in police investigations.

BIBLIOGRAPHY

Howitt, D. (2018). Introduction to forensic and criminal psychology. Essex, UK: Pearson. 6th edition.

Brown, J., Shell, Y. & Cole, T. (2015). Forensic Psychology: Theory, research, policy and practice. 1st edition

Wood, J. & Gannon, T.A. (2009). Public opinion and criminal justice. Devon, UK: Willan Publishing.

Thank you for reading.

I hoped you enjoyed it.

If you want a FREE book and keep up to date about new books and project. Then please sign up for my newsletter at www.connorwhiteley.net/

Have a great day.

CHECK OUT THE PSYCHOLOGY WORLD PODCAST FOR MORE PSYCHOLOGY INFORMATION!

AVAILABLE ON ALL MAJOR PODCAST APPS.

About the author:

Connor Whiteley is the author of over 30 books in the sci-fi fantasy, nonfiction psychology and books for writer's genre and he is a Human Branding Speaker and Consultant.

He is a passionate Warhammer 40,000 reader, psychology student and author.

Who narrates his own audiobooks and he hosts The Psychology World Podcast.

All whilst studying Psychology at the University of Kent, England.

Also, he was a former Explorer Scout where he gave a speech to the Maltese President in August 2018 and he attended Prince Charles' 70th Birthday Party at Buckingham Palace in May 2018.

Plus, he is a self-confessed coffee lover!

Please follow me on:

Website: www.connorwhiteley.net

Twitter: @scifiwhiteley

Please leave on honest review as this helps with the discoverability of the book and I truly appreciate it.

Thank you for reading. I hope you've enjoyed it.

CRIMINAL PROFILING

All books in 'An Introductory Series':

BIOLOGICAL PSYCHOLOGY 3RD EDITION

COGNITIVE PSYCHOLOGY 2ND EDITION

SOCIAL PSYCHOLOGY- 3RD EDITION

ABNORMAL PSYCHOLOGY 3RD EDITION

PSYCHOLOGY OF RELATIONSHIPS-3RD EDITION

DEVELOPMENTAL PSYCHOLOGY 3RD EDITION

HEALTH PSYCHOLOGY

RESEARCH IN PSYCHOLOGY

A GUIDE TO MENTAL HEALTH AND TREATMENT AROUND THE WORLD-A GLOBAL LOOK AT DEPRESSION

FORENSIC PSYCHOLOGY

THE FORENSIC PSYCHOLOGY OF THEFT, BURGLARY AND OTHER

RIMES AGAINST PROPERTY

CRIMINAL PROFILING: A FORENSIC
PSYCHOLOGY GUIDE TO FBI
PROFILING AND GEOGRAPHICAL
AND STATISTICAL PROFILING.

CLINICAL PSYCHOLOGY

FORMULATION IN PSYCHOTHERAPY

Companion guides:

BIOLOGICAL PSYCHOLOGY 2ND
EDITION WORKBOOK

COGNITIVE PSYCHOLOGY 2ND
EDITION WORKBOOK

SOCIOCULTURAL PSYCHOLOGY 2ND
EDITION WORKBOOK

ABNORMAL PSYCHOLOGY 2ND
EDITION WORKBOOK

PSYCHOLOGY OF HUMAN
RELATIONSHIPS 2ND EDITION
WORKBOOK

HEALTH PSYCHOLOGY WORKBOOK

FORENSIC PSYCHOLOGY WORKBOOK

OTHER SHORT STORIES BY CONNOR WHITELEY

Blade of The Emperor

Arbiter's Truth

The Bloodied Rose

Asmodia's Wrath

Other books by Connor Whiteley:

THE ANGEL OF RETURN

THE ANGEL OF FREEDOM

GARRO: GALAXY'S END

GARRO: RISE OF THE ORDER

GARRO: END TIMES

GARRO: SHORT STORIES

GARRO: COLLECTION

GARRO: HERESY

GARRO: FAITHLESS

GARRO: DESTROYER OF WORLDS

Audiobooks by Connor Whiteley:

BIOLOGICAL PSYCHOLOGY

COGNITIVE PSYCHOLOGY

SOCIOCULTURAL PSYCHOLOGY

ABNORMAL PSYCHOLOGY

PSYCHOLOGY OF HUMAN
RELATIONSHIPS

HEALTH PSYCHOLOGY

DEVELOPMENTAL PSYCHOLOGY

RESEARCH IN PSYCHOLOGY

FORENSIC PSYCHOLOGY

GARRO: GALAXY'S END

GARRO: RISE OF THE ORDER

GARRO: SHORT STORIES

GARRO: END TIMES

GARRO: COLLECTION

GARRO: HERESY

GARRO: FAITHLESS

GARRO: DESTROYER OF WORLDS

GARRO: COLLECTION BOOKS 4-6

GARRO: COLLECTION BOOKS 1-6

Business books:

TIME MANAGEMENT: A GUIDE FOR
STUDENTS AND WORKERS

LEADERSHIP: WHAT MAKES A GOOD
LEADER? A GUIDE FOR STUDENTS
AND WORKERS.

BUSINESS SKILLS: HOW TO SURVIVE
THE BUSINESS WORLD? A GUIDE FOR
STUDENTS, EMPLOYEES AND
EMPLOYERS.

BUSINESS COLLECTION

GET YOUR FREE BOOK AT:
WWW.CONNORWHITELEY.NET

Printed in Great Britain
by Amazon

20364960R00058